118622

7h
11/10
8-63

AL life
GUIDES

Real Life Guide to Childcare

This first edition published in 2009 by Trotman Publishing, an imprint of Crimson Publishing, Westminster House, Kew Road, Richmond, Surrey TW9 2ND

Author: Caroline Barker

British Library Cataloguing in Publication Data
A catalogue record for this book is available from the British Library

ISBN: 978-1-84455-221-4

Typeset by RefineCatch Ltd, Bungay, Suffolk

Printed and bound in Italy by LEGO SpA

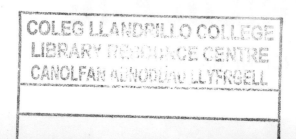

CONTENTS

FOREWORD

This *Real Life Guide to Childcare* offers practical information on every aspect of training for and finding a job in the field. Whether you are just starting out or looking for your next career move, this book shows the different entry routes into the industry, gives you an outline of the jobs available, and explains the skills and attributes you need to be successful.

City & Guilds vocational qualifications support learners from pre-entry to professional level and we award over a million certificates every year. Our qualifications meet the latest industry requirements and are recognised by employers worldwide as proof that candidates have the knowledge and skills to get the job done.

We are delighted to be a part of the Trotman *Real Life Guides* series to help raise your awareness of these vocational qualifications – we are confident that they can help you to achieve excellence and quality in whichever field you choose. For more information about the courses City & Guilds offer, check out www.cityandguilds.com – get yourself qualified and see what you could do.

City & Guilds

ABOUT THE AUTHOR

Caroline Barker is a professionally qualified careers adviser
with many years' experience of providing careers guidance and
counselling services to a wide range of clients. She has worked
with school pupils, apprenticeship trainees, college students, and
adults seeking a career change.

Seeking a career change herself, she moved into working as a
freelance writer and research consultant, specialising in the fields
of careers, education and training. In this capacity she has worked
for various careers publishers including Cascaid, VT Careers
Management, AGCAS, and Lifetime Publishing, as well as Sector
Skills Council Skillset.

Her work at present is predominantly geared towards young
people. She is committed to producing accurate and engaging
careers information for this readership, enabling them to make
informed choices about their future career.

Caroline is a full member of the Institute of Career Guidance, a
member of the Careers Writers' Association, an affiliate member
of the Institute for Learning, and a conference member of
AGCAS.

She is also the author of *Real Life Guide: The Police Service, 2nd
edition* published by Trotman.

ACKNOWLEDGEMENTS

Many thanks to all the case study interviewees who gave up their time to discuss their careers and offer their honest opinions: Jacqueline Johnson from Nottingham City Council, Jonny Hoyle from North Yorkshire County Council, Nik Owen from Kaleidoscope Day Nurseries, Paulette Otete (a childminder), Dave Scott from Fulford School, and Lynn Owen-Jones from Nottingham Community Health. Hopefully I've conveyed their commitment to their jobs, and to making a difference, within their case studies.

INTRODUCTION

If you are considering a career working with children and young people then this book has been written for you. You may be thinking what skills would I need for a successful career in this field? What jobs are available? What are the career opportunities? The aim of the book is to help you decide whether working in the childcare sector, more recently referred to as the children's workforce, is really the career for you.

If you work or volunteer with children, young people and their families then you are a member of the children's workforce. This workforce spans a number of different sectors, and you could be working as a nursery worker in an early years setting or as a social worker within children's social care. You could also be working in youth work, in education or in the health sector. This book aims to explain more about working in the main core of the children's workforce, which covers jobs where working with children and young people is the main focus of your job, rather than part of your job.

Chapter 2 (What's the Story?) explains more about what the children's workforce is, and what recent developments there have been in this field. In recent years there have been fundamental changes to government policy that have led to raising the profile of jobs in this workforce, which is a very positive thing, not only for children in general but also for people looking towards this as a career!

Chapter 4 (Tools of the Trade) focuses on the variety of skills and personal qualities you will need to work with children and young people, with the aim of finding out if you've got what it takes. If you have, then Chapter 6 (What are the Jobs?) gives you a better idea of the roles within the different sectors that you may choose to work in, and what you would be doing in these roles.

Chapter 8 (FAQs) answers the kind of questions you may be wondering about, such as who will I work for and what can I expect to earn, and Chapter 10 (Training and Qualifications) looks at the different kinds of qualifications you may want to consider and the kind of training you may go on to do. Finally, Chapter 12 (The Last Word) summarises what the book is all about, and Chapter 13 (Further Information) gives you details of relevant organisations that may be useful if you want to do some more research.

Real-life case studies will show you what people in a variety of different roles within the sectors actually think about their jobs. Read the case studies carefully, as they will give you an insight into the person behind the job, and the attitude and personal qualities that have helped them succeed. A common theme is the motivation to make a difference to children's lives – to help them achieve their potential as they move from early years, through school and into adolescence and adulthood.

Do you think you can make a difference? Read on, and learn about the various roles you can undertake within the children's workforce that will make a difference to every child, young person and the families you may work with.

CHAPTER 1
SUCCESS STORY

JACQUELINE JOHNSON

Acting Team Manager

Jacqueline Johnson is an Acting Team Manager within leaving care services* for Nottingham City Council. Having been the acting team manager for leaving care she has temporarily been seconded to acting team manager for a team of personal advisers.

Jacqueline has been committed to working with children and young people for 20 years. Even when she was very young she remembers saying to her mother, 'I want to look after children and I want children of all cultures to live together happily.' Jacqueline trained and worked as a nursery nurse before becoming a social worker. She has also fostered a young person for a number of years, provided respite (temporary) foster care to a number of young people, and also managed to squeeze in working at weekends for a number of years at a homeless hostel for 16–25-year-olds.

As a mother of three young children herself Jacqueline was shocked by the negative attitudes of some of the local people and

---

*Leaving care services provide advice, support and assistance to young people who are leaving the care system (eg foster care/residential care). They support young people aged 16 to 21 years (24 if in education) in gaining the necessary skills to live independently as they enter into adulthood.

parents towards children within her local community. 'They were seen and not heard, sworn and shouted at.' This motivated her to make a difference. 'It's all about making a difference to a child's life because children are our future. I'd like to be remembered by young people as the one who always said don't give up.'

Jacqueline went back to college, completed an NNEB (National Nursery Examination Board) Diploma in Nursery Nursing and gained Adult Learner of the Year Award. She worked as a nursery nurse for Barnardo's organising activities for 3–5-year-olds in an inner city community-based nursery, working with children from a diverse range of cultural and socio-economic backgrounds. She then went on to manage the West Indian's Nations Association (WINA) nursery, another community-based initiative, which involved setting up and running the nursery from its beginning.

During this time Jacqueline became more interested in social work, did some voluntary work in a residential home, and went on to become an unqualified social worker in children and looked after a team. 'I felt I had done as much as I could as a nursery nurse and it seemed a natural progression to move into social work.' She went on to take the Diploma in Social Work and helped establish a new leaving care team, following the implementation of the Children (Leaving Care) Act 2000.

After qualifying and gaining more experience she became an Assistant Team Manager before Acting Team Manager. Jacqueline's role was to liaise between the manager and the other workers, including social workers and personal advisers. Her aim was to assist young people in getting their wishes and feelings heard, continue to develop the team and to make sure they stayed young-person focused. She also still had her own caseload of young people leaving the care system.

As a way of consulting with care leavers the team set up the 'Care-free' group which involves a number of care leavers editing a magazine to put their views across on issues such as Black History

Month, International Women's Day, Chinese New Year, as well as producing everyday information about jobs, benefits and even cooking!

Jacqueline was responsible for organising an Achievement Event during National Care Leavers' Week that takes place annually. This included approaching local organisations to act as ambassadors and champions for care leavers, in their role as corporate parents. This sees local government and businesses working together in promoting better outcomes for young people in and leaving the care system. A local building firm took on a number of trainees while other organisations assisted in the organising of a care leavers' ball. The awards were based on the '5 Outcomes' (see Chapter 2) and were presented to those who had achieved within one or more of these. Achievements could range from academic success, maintaining a tenancy or passing a driving test. An award named after Samantha Morton, the Nottingham-born actress who was a care leaver, was devised for outstanding achievement.

Currently acting as team manager to a team of personal advisers, Jacqueline is responsible for making sure the workers are completing a young persons' 'Pathway Plan' in line with legislation and taking into account the young persons' wishes and feelings. Pathway plans look at issues including education, training and employment, accommodation, finances and identity. It is the duty of a local authority to keep in touch with young people leaving care, and it has to demonstrate how this is done, even for those who may not want to engage!

Jacqueline is very positive about her job and passionate about the leaving care service. 'I like making a difference to people's lives. I like the fact that young people can make mistakes and we as a corporate parent can never say leave and never come back.' She also stresses the importance for social workers to realise that as a corporate parent they need to think 'is this good enough?' while at the same time maintaining an appropriate professional relationship.

The main qualities a social worker needs, Jacqueline believes, are: 'To have a drive and develop your own individual style of working, and not to give up. You've got to be approachable and be able to engage with young people at all levels. You also need common sense and to be determined, versatile and young-people focused.'

Social work managers face different challenges: 'As a manager you need to keep budgets, and to keep workers, young people and the powers above happy.' After gaining more management experience Jacqueline would like to move into a more developmental role within the service.

Jacqueline's top tip for any young person starting out on their career is to: 'Never give up. Have a plan of what you want to do and if you don't get it the first time, then try again. See every small step as a success and not a failure, because you have changed your life in a positive way. The more you widen your scope in life then nothing is wasted.'

CHAPTER 2
WHAT'S THE STORY?

You may think in today's society that children are well looked after, safe from harm and are happy in their lives. Unfortunately this isn't always the case for a number of reasons, from family separation or not achieving at school to being bullied or being abused by parents or carers.

Back in the early nineteenth century, however, before the Government made a series of reforms to protect children, things were a lot worse. Many children were forced to work at an early age and were homeless and living in poverty, with no support from people such as teachers or social workers.

The 1870s saw a dramatic change in the promotion of children's welfare, with the introduction of new laws that prevented children from working in factories or as chimney sweeps, and allowed them for the first time to have a right to education. The pioneering work of people such as Dr Thomas Barnardo enabled children to emerge from 'being seen and not heard' to actually having more say in their lifestyles. This led to a new era in 'looking after' children that would shape the way in how we view children today.

Fast-forward to the twenty-first century – we now have various Children's Acts giving more rights and opportunities for children to excel in their lives and achieve the best possible outcomes irrespective of their backgrounds, ability, race or gender. We also have a government agenda focusing on how children can achieve their potential as children and adults in the future. These include forming a designated children's workforce.

THE CHILDREN'S WORKFORCE

If you work with children, young people and their families, whether in paid employment or voluntary work, then you are a member of the children's workforce. This workforce stretches across many professional and organisational boundaries and includes early years/childcare workers, teachers, nurses, social workers, youth workers and many other people.

In recent years there have been fundamental changes in government policy and legislation that have had a major impact on everyone in the children's workforce and have led to raising the profile of jobs in this workforce.

EVERY CHILD MATTERS

In 2003 the Government published the Green Paper Every Child Matters. This was published alongside the formal response to the report into the tragic death of Victoria Climbie. Victoria was an 8-year-old girl who was horrifically abused and tortured and eventually killed by her great-aunt and the man they lived with. One of the aims of Every Child Matters was to make sure that a tragedy like this does not happen again.

The Green Paper led to a huge debate about services for children, young people and their families. People working in children's services, and parents, children and young people were all consulted on their views on how children and young people should be treated and helped. This led to the passing of the Children Act 2004 and the publishing of Every Child Matters: Change for Children in November 2004.

Every Child Matters: Change for Children is a new approach to make sure children and young people from birth to 19, whatever their background or their circumstances, can have a good life. The Government's aim is for every child to have the support they need to:

▶ be healthy
▶ stay safe
▶ enjoy and achieve
▶ make a positive contribution
▶ achieve economic well-being.

These five aims are at the heart of the Children Act 2004. This has led to organisations involved with providing services to children and young people teaming up in new ways and working together to protect children and young people from harm and to help them achieve their potential. The Government also appointed a Children's Commissioner for England in 2005, to give children and young people a voice in government and public life.

CHILDREN'S WORKFORCE DEVELOPMENT COUNCIL

The Children's Workforce Development Council (CWDC) was set up in 2005 to support the implementation of Every Child Matters. It works in the interest of a range of sectors and supports over 500,000 people in the children's workforce working with children, young people, families and carers across England. Of these 500,000 workers, 80% are employed and 20% are self-employed. It also supports around 250,000 volunteers. As a sector skills council body they aim to address the skills needs of workers in their footprint, ie the types of workers they represent.

Workers in their footprint include people working in early years provision (for example early years practitioners in nurseries and pre-schools) and those involved in children's social care provision (such as social workers and family support workers). Their footprint also covers workers in supportive roles working primarily with 13–19-year-olds, such as education welfare officers and learning mentors. They do not, however, cover all people who work with children in their job. Teachers and health service professionals, for example, are not covered by their remit.

The CWDC therefore works closely with colleagues in the Children's Workforce Network (CWN) to address common issues across the whole of the children's workforce. The CWN brings together people working with children and young people in health, social care, education, justice, youth work, play and other related areas. The CWN has developed a work plan that aims to make sure that staff working with children have the right skills and knowledge, that they work together well, and that they have access to clear career paths both within and across the different sectors.

CHILDREN'S WORKFORCE STRATEGY

In December 2008 the Government published the 2020 Children and Young People's Workforce Strategy. This sets out the Government's vision that everyone who works with children and young people should be:

▶ ambitious for every child and young person
▶ excellent in their practice

▶ committed to partnership and integrated working

▶ respected and valued as professionals.

The change in children's services outlined in Every Child Matters provides the context for the Children's Workforce Strategy, which aims to develop a world class workforce to improve outcomes for young people. This identified four main strategic challenges.

▶ Recruiting more people into the children's workforce.

▶ Developing and retaining more people in the workforce.

▶ Strengthening integrated working and developing new workforce roles.

▶ Improving and strengthening leadership, management and supervision.

A CHANGING WORKFORCE

In 2004, Choice for Parents, the Best Start for Children: A ten year strategy for childcare set out the Government's plans to make early learning and childcare in England truly world class. The first ever Childcare Act in 2006 also gave local authorities responsibility for increasing childcare places in order to meet the demands of childcare locally.

As a result the early years and childcare sector is rapidly expanding, and there has never been a better time to start working with young children. A national early years and childcare recruitment campaign 'Working in Early Years. It's not just child's play' was launched in 2007 to inspire all people to take up careers in early years and childcare. They particularly want to recruit people from minority ethnic backgrounds who will have wider community and cultural benefits, and to encourage young men to think about a career working with children, in roles that have traditionally been seen as jobs for women. The sector is highly female dominated – in day nursery settings only 2% of the

DID YOU KNOW?

Almost 2.3 million children and their families can now use one of almost 3,000 children's centres providing access to early learning and childcare, maternity and child health services.

Source: *The Next Steps for Early Learning and Childcare*, HM Government (January 2009)

staff are male, and also under-represented by black, minority ethnic workers at 9% of all staff (source: 'Occupational summary sheet: Early Years workers in day nurseries', revised 2007–8, CWDC). The aim is to challenge perceptions and change attitudes.

Changes are under way across the whole workforce. In April 2008 the Government published Building Brighter Futures: Next Steps for the Children's Workforce. In a commitment to improving and developing the children's workforce it pledged to invest £305 million in early years, £25 million in the youth workforce, £7.5 million in the play workforce, as well as nearly £73 million in a package of proposals to support social workers working with children and young people. The Government's aim is to recruit more high quality staff into the children's workforce and then retain them by offering better development and career progression. So if you're looking at a career in this area then there's never been a more exciting time!

Before you move on to Case Study 1 (Chapter 3) and then to Chapter 4, which focuses on the main skills needed to work with children and young people, why not take a few minutes to do the quick quiz opposite? The aim of the quiz is to test your knowledge and see just how much you really know about the children's workforce.

QUIZ

---

1 **Why do 2,500 children and young people phone Childline each day?**
A. Because they are being bullied
B. Because they are being abused
C. Because of family problems

---

2 **Who opened the first children's home in 1867?**
A. Dr Seuss
B. Dr Barnardo
C. Dr Pepper

---

3 **What is the percentage of male workers in Early Years?**
A. 60%
B. 25%
C. 2%

---

4 **What is 'safeguarding'?**
A. Keeping children safe from harm
B. A new sport for the 2012 Olympics
C. A security officer's role in a bank

---

5 **The children's workforce is the collective term for?**
A. All children who are employed
B. All people who work with children, young people and their families
C. All children who are no longer in education

6 **Which of the following is NOT one of the five aims of Every Child Matters? For every child to have the support they need to:**

A. Be healthy

B. Stay safe

C. Be happy

7 **How many people are in the children's workforce represented by the CWDC?**

A. 200,000

B. 500,000

C. 1 million

ANSWERS

1. All three! Childline is available 24 hours a day, all year round and offers advice and counselling on anything that is bothering you!

2. B. Dr Barnardo pioneered reforms in child welfare during Victorian times and opened 96 homes before his death in 1905. The Barnardo's charity carries on his work today on a worldwide scale.

3. C. Male workers and people from minority ethnic backgrounds are hugely under-represented in the early years sector and across the children's workforce as a whole.

4. A. The Children Act 1989 (section 17) states it is the duty of a local authority to 'safeguard and promote the welfare of children living in their area'.

5. B. The children's workforce covers everyone who works (whether paid or as a volunteer) with children, young people and their families. It includes people such as nurses, teachers, youth workers and midwives among many others.

6. C. Be happy. While being happy is important to all children's lives, it is not one of the five aims of Every Child Matters.

7. B. The CWDC supports over 500,000 people in the children's workforce working with children, young people, families and carers across England.

THE NATIONAL SOCIETY FOR THE PREVENTION OF CRUELTY TO CHILDREN (NSPCC)

We have 180 community-based projects and run the NSPCC Helpline and Childline in the UK and the Channel Islands.

Our aim:
We want to see a society where all children are loved, valued and able to fulfil their potential. To do this, we have 4 objectives.

1. To mobilise everyone to take action to end child cruelty.
2. To give children the help, support and environment they need to stay safe from cruelty.
3. To find ways of working with communities to keep children safe from cruelty.
4. To be, and be seen as, someone to turn to for children and young people.

Source: NSPCC website www.nspcc.org.uk

CHAPTER 3
CASE STUDY 1

JONNY HOYLE

Family Support Worker

Jonny Hoyle works as a Family Support Worker for North Yorkshire County Council. He is based in a family support team within children's social care in Scarborough.

Jonny is also currently Chairman for A National Voice, a charity run for and by young people who are or have been in care.

As a care leaver himself Jonny feels he didn't actually choose this career, rather it chose him. He was receiving services from the leaving care service in Scarborough when an opportunity to apply for a post within leaving care came up. It was for a care leaver to work with and support other care leavers. He applied and was in the temporary post for 18 months. He was particularly involved in participation and consultation – getting looked-after children and care leavers involved in what they want from the service – and then looking at making improvements.

During this time Jonny became involved with A National Voice, at the time a pilot organisation funded by the Prince's Trust. He got a job with them as a regional development worker, and was seconded to the leaving care team in Scarborough.

⌕ DID YOU KNOW?

A National Voice was set up in 1999 and is a charity run by care-experienced young people, providing a voice for the 60,000 looked-after children and young people to help improve the care system.

Source: A National Voice website www.anationalvoice.org

'I liked the idea of a young person led organisation. This was the same sort of work but on a much bigger scale. I was in touch with groups of looked-after children and care leavers and speaking on a national level about what they wanted. I spoke at the Association of Directors of Children's Services conference, and was a member of the All Party Parliamentary Committee for Looked After Children. It was a chance to influence policy by telling ministers what young people were telling me.'

Jonny then made the decision that working in children's social care was what he really wanted to do so he applied to be a family support worker. 'I'm passionate about making a difference and wanted to do whatever I could do to make a difference. Getting a job directly working with children and families seemed a good way in.

'My role as a family support worker really is what it says on the tin. I support families with a real focus on improving the lives of children and their families. I aim to see all my families weekly or fortnightly, to identify problems and then identify solutions to those problems. This may involve, for example, setting achievable targets with children around school attendance or mediating between children and parents over what time they should come home at night.'

Jonny works closely with social workers and other professionals, such as education welfare officers and home school support workers, and other agencies such as the youth justice service and the police, with the aim of working together to deal with the issues facing families. He works a lot with teenagers with challenging behaviour. Issues may be about reducing offending, increasing attendance at school, or setting boundaries.

A typical day? 'There isn't one! I could be rolling around in a sandpit or playing games with a toddler in the morning and playing pool or football with a teenager in the afternoon. Or I could be popping into a school to check that a child has arrived on time, running a parenting class or attending a child protection case conference. So you need to be flexible.

'You also need to be child focused, which means you need to be approachable and friendly. You need to be honest and clear with families so they understand exactly who we are, what we do, and the consequences of their actions. You need to be really assertive at times, for example on days when you have to remove children from their families. If a child is at risk of significant harm then we have a duty to ensure the safety of the child.'

Jonny really enjoys his job: 'The reason I'm in this job is to make a difference to children's lives and parents' lives so seeing that difference is the best part of the job by far. When you build up relationships with young people you are effectively shaping their lives. You may see someone get back into school and sit exams, for example. I recently sat down with a young person and his family and we looked back at how much they had all moved on in the last few years, and they thanked me for the work I had done. There's a lot of hard work involved in this job but it brings you the rewards that money can't buy.

'Some days, however, it can be the worst job in the world. When you're working with particularly challenging families who either don't want to change or don't have the ability to change. It's particularly sad if you have to end up removing a child despite all the work you may have done.

'The biggest challenge to family support workers is effecting change. No two cases are the same, no two families are the same and no two kids are the same. We have to get the level of support right for them all. Another challenge is to change people's perceptions of us, as typically people don't want the stigmatisation of being involved with us.'

Jonny has applied to take a social work degree and aims to become a social worker.

'I'd like to effect as much change as I can to as many children and young people as I can.' In order to do this he may look towards becoming a manager or go into policy. He'd like to top off his career back in the voluntary sector, 'Eventually I'd like to be a chief executive of a charity like A National Voice!'

Jonny's tips for anyone wanting to work with children are to give it a try first. 'Get some experience, do some voluntary work and see if you like it. Then really the sky's the limit – know where you want to end up and do whatever you can to get there.'

CHAPTER 4
TOOLS OF THE TRADE

As part of the Every Child Matters agenda (see Chapter 2), a new framework has been developed which sets out what skills and knowledge you will need to work effectively with children, young people and their families. This is known as The Common Core of Skills and Knowledge for the Children's Workforce – often referred to as 'The Common Core'. The skills and knowledge included in the Common Core have been sub-divided into 6 areas:

1. effective communication with children, young people and their families
2. child and young person development
3. safeguarding and promoting the welfare of the child
4. supporting transitions
5. multi agency working
6. sharing information.

This chapter focuses on the key skills, abilities and personal qualities that are important to a career working with children and young people. Some of these you may already have and some you may need to develop further if you decide that a career in the children's workforce is the career for you.

EFFECTIVE COMMUNICATION WITH CHILDREN, YOUNG PEOPLE AND THEIR FAMILIES

Good communication is central to working with children and young people. Effective communication is not just about talking to people. It involves listening, questioning, understanding and responding to what is being communicated by others. Think about how well you communicate.

- ▶ Can you actively listen in a calm, open and non-threatening manner?
- ▶ Do you use questions to check you have fully understood what people are saying, and that they have understood you?
- ▶ Can you consult with children and young people and consider their opinions?

In order to engage effectively, you will need to think about what form of communication is most appropriate for who you are working with, paying close attention to their age, ability and understanding.

Having respect and empathy

Q DID YOU KNOW?

In the past we have run initiatives to help young adults to get involved in their communities. To date, there have already been almost 200,000 young people involved in over 130 project locations in England.
Source: CSV website
www.csv.org.uk/volunteer

Another aspect to effective communication is to build an appropriate relationship based on respect and honesty. It is important to be open and honest with children and their families as this develops a sense of trust and ensures that they feel valued, leading to improved communication and better outcomes. This sense of respect combined with empathy and an understanding of the issues, concerns and interests of the child/family you are working with will help you engage more effectively.

Information recording skills

As well as the above skills, an ability to be able to record information is essential. You may be asked to produce a report about your work, so making sure information is written down in a clear, concise and factual way is important.

If you want to improve your communication skills then any kind of voluntary work with children and young people would help.

CHILD AND YOUNG PERSON DEVELOPMENT

In order to be able to work effectively with children and young people, it is important to have knowledge and understanding of how they grow and develop physically, emotionally and socially. There is no magical guide to why and how people develop, because everyone is different. What we do know, though, is that people's experiences, both positive and negative, can affect how they develop during childhood – this may be seen through their physical health, their relationships with friends and family or their behaviour. It is important therefore to realise and understand how changes within a child's life can impact on their day-to-day and future development.

DID YOU KNOW?

90% of a child's brain connections will be made by the time they are 5. That means that their development and learning from birth to the age of 5 has a significant influence on their future lives.
Source: CWDC website
www.cwdcouncil.org.uk

Observational skills

In this context, observation skills are essential. You may have to observe how a child interacts with other children or adults or whether their physical development is similar to other children of a similar age. For example, when working with babies or very young children it is important to have an understanding of whether they are meeting certain targets. These are referred to as developmental milestones and include, for example, whether a baby can crawl at a certain age. If these milestones are not being met, it could be due to a lack of stimulation from the parents, an indication of a development delay or undiagnosed disability, or it could just be that everyone is different!

Engaging with the child, their parents and carers

Through engaging with the child and their parents or carers, you will gain a better understanding of why some changes in development and behaviour happen. Behaviour may change unexpectedly in a child as a result of a house move, change of school or family upset. It is important to recognise these changes, as they can be a sign of something more significant in the child's life, such as whether they are being bullied or are suffering significant harm or abuse.

Using your own life experiences

Another key skill used in this area is the ability to use your own experiences in resolving what the issue may be. Remember that even your own life experiences can be of help when working with children. You may be able to empathise and understand a change in a child's behaviour if you have experienced something similar yourself. Think and reflect on what was going on in your life at the time, how did you deal with it and would you do it differently?

By using these skills you will be able to motivate and encourage children and young people to reach their full potential, as well as empower their parents or carers at the same time.

SAFEGUARDING AND PROMOTING THE WELFARE OF THE CHILD

Safeguarding is about keeping children safe from harm and abuse. This means keeping children safe from accidents, abuse and bullying and actively promoting their well-being in a healthy, safe and supportive environment. It is the responsibility of every local authority to 'safeguard and promote the welfare of a child living within their area' (Source: s.17 Children Act 1989).

Integrated working

Safeguarding is an important part of integrated working. When professionals work together in an integrated way, they put the child at the centre of all activities to help identify their needs earlier in order to enhance and improve their life outcomes. Early intervention can help children and families back on track and avoid problems turning into a crisis. Every adult who works with a child or young person has a duty to safeguard and promote their welfare.

Being open and honest

In this context it is vital that you have a trusting and respectful relationship with the child and their parents or carers. You may be in a potentially confrontational situation so being open and honest is key to making sure that any issue regarding a child suffering significant harm is dealt with quickly and appropriately. Both the child and their parents or carers need to be informed about what is happening and be involved, wherever possible, in any decision-making.

Being able to make difficult decisions

Safeguarding can be a very tricky area to deal with. You may face difficult decisions that may impact on your future work with the

DID YOU KNOW?

Every 10 days in England and
Wales one child is killed at the
hands of their parent.
Source: Home Office (2007)

child and their family. The most
important thing to remember is
the 'welfare of the child is always
paramount' (Source: Welfare
Checklist, Children Act 1989).
It is your considered judgement
about when and how to act in
order to safeguard and promote a
child's or young person's welfare. Safeguarding children can be a
very demanding and stressful aspect to your work, so you need to
be aware of how this may affect you emotionally and think about
ways of coping with this.

SUPPORTING TRANSITIONS

As they grow and develop, children and young people will
go through a number of changes. For example, a move from
primary to secondary school, a house move to a different area,
or a family break-up. These changes are known as transitions
and can have a massive impact on development, behaviour and
the child's ability to cope with such a change. It is therefore
important to:

▶ build positive relationships with children, parents and carers in
order to understand what impact these transitions may have on
the family you are working with

▶ develop your skills in empathy in order to relate to what might
be happening for everyone, not just the child or young person,
at that particular time.

MULTI-AGENCY WORKING

Multi-agency working is about the many different services,
agencies and staff within the children's workforce working
together to provide a holistic service that meets the needs of

children, young people and their families. In order for this to work successfully, you will need to:

▶ know about how your own role fits in with the wider service
▶ understand when you might need to bring in support from another agency
▶ communicate effectively with other professionals and agencies, making sure you listen to advice but also making sure that you are listened to as well.

SHARING INFORMATION

Different agencies need to work together and share information to ensure the safety and well-being of children. You will, therefore, also need to:

▶ know when and how to share information, as it could ultimately save someone's life
▶ have an understanding of the laws linked to information sharing
▶ be clear about what information can be shared and with whom.

In this chapter we have looked at some of the main skills and personal qualities needed in working with children, young people and their families. Think about whether you have these skills already or how you can develop and improve these further, for example through voluntary work, undertaking a course, or through general life experience. Have a look at the case studies throughout the book and reflect on how these skills are put into practice. Whichever role you go into, you will need to use the above skills and knowledge effectively. Above all, you will need to have energy and enthusiasm for what you do – together with an endless amount of patience – in order to meet the needs of the child or family you are working with.

CHAPTER 5
CASE STUDY 2

NIK OWEN

Nursery Manager

Nik Owen works for Kaleidoscope Day Nurseries. He is the manager of their city centre site in York and also manages two of their local out-of-school clubs.

Within the nursery Nik manages 18 staff, including assistant childcare practitioners, childcare practitioners, an early years coordinator and a cook. All the childcare staff are either qualified child carers or working towards such a qualification. The nursery has specialist rooms for babies and toddlers, areas for creative activities, areas for quiet play, and preschool teaching. There is also a large walled garden. Each room has a room supervisor responsible for not only the room but also the staff within the room.

Nik is responsible for supporting the staff, while they are responsible for supporting the children. Nik's role as a manager, however, has become increasingly policy based. He needs to make sure the nursery is following all the national strategies introduced by the Government. In September 2008, for example, the Government introduced the Early Years Foundation Stage (EYFS), a new framework for learning, development and care for children from birth to 5, which all nurseries must now follow.

Nik is responsible for implementing the EYFS in the nursery and supporting the new framework.

'Each child has a Learning Journey to complete during their time at nursery and a key worker who records and monitors their progress in their Learning Journey. The Early Years Coordinator, who has Qualified Teacher Status, is specifically responsible for coordinating the EYFS with pre-school children aged 2 to 5 years.'

In terms of staff support Nik has regular staff meetings and supervisor meetings, and monthly supervisions with the room supervisors. He spends at least one morning a week with the children in the nursery, and also does regular walk-arounds, chatting with the children and staff to make sure everything is running smoothly. 'Because we're working with children we have to work as a team and everyone has a voice. We discuss issues and reflect on what we're doing. I encourage staff to take constructive criticism and to help them develop in their roles.'

Nik has an annual and monthly budget and deals with all the financial aspects of the nursery, such as invoicing and collecting fees, and buying in food, resources and training. He collects weekly figures for the owner of the nursery on how many children have been in the nursery that week. He also puts bids in to the local council for grants, and has recently applied for IT equipment and outdoor provision.

It was not a difficult career choice for Nik. 'I always knew I wanted to work with children. My sister has cerebral palsy so I did voluntary work for SNAPPY (Special Needs Activities and Play Provision for York), a voluntary organisation for children with special needs, working on their holiday and weekend playschemes while I was at school. I also did my work experience in two special schools in York.

'I left school at 16 and took an NNEB certificate at college which qualified me to Level 2. During the course I had a placement in a baby room and really enjoyed it. I then started working in a small nursery in their baby unit, took an NVQ Level 3 in Childcare and Education, and worked my way up to assistant manager. I also did a course to become the Special Educational Needs Coordinator (SENCO) for the nursery, identifying and supporting children with special needs. I went on to become a manager of another nursery, then came here as Deputy Manager, and took over as Manager six months ago.'

In line with government policy all nursery managers will soon be expected to have a degree or be working towards one, and Nik is currently taking a Foundation degree in Supporting Learning, which will lead on to the final year of an Honours degree in Education Studies.

What Nik really enjoys about his job is: 'Every day is different. I never thought I could do an office-based job because I like being busy, which is why I chose to work in a nursery, but I am very busy now! Also I came into this work to make a difference, and on the management side this is even more relevant. Everything you do in this job makes a difference to the children.'

The main challenges in his job are: 'I believe that children should be allowed to be children and play but we have to try and balance that with what the Government wants us to do, including statutory requirements such as the EYFS, which involves tying children down to a lot of observations and assessments. So we allow the children to do what they want, and base our work around that.'

The important skills and qualities needed to work with children in early years, Nik believes, are: 'You need to be able to multi-task, be patient and have a degree of common sense. You need to be able to see the bigger picture, for example with the EYFS, and adapt what is needed to best suit the children. You also need the ability to listen, both to the children and to other staff.'

While Nik is very happy in his present role he is considering various options for the future: 'I've looked into becoming an OFSTED inspector. I also like the idea of development work. Local authorities have development workers supporting nurseries and schools, and children's centres have similar workers supporting people accessing the centres.'

Nik's tips to someone looking to work in early years are: 'You can do a college-based route or a work-based route to become qualified, and this really depends on whether you're academic or more hands-on. Work experience is usually the first step but it can be a positive experience or a nightmare depending on where you do your placement, so don't let it put you off. Think about doing some voluntary work as well.'

CHAPTER 6
WHAT ARE THE JOBS?

In this chapter we focus on who does what within the children's workforce, covering work with children and young people in a variety of settings. As we saw earlier, this workforce spans a number of different sectors and therefore there are many different types of jobs to consider. But what are the jobs? And what would you be doing in them? This chapter covers work in early years, children's social care, CAFCASS, youth justice, the young people's workforce, the school workforce, educational psychology and relevant jobs in health. Take a look at the following jobs within these sectors and what you might be doing in them.

EARLY YEARS

Early years workers/practitioners work in a wide range of childcare settings, including day nurseries, nursery schools and primary schools, pre-schools/playgroups, out-of-school settings, and children's centres which provide a range of services for families and children up to the age of 5. They also work in home-based childcare, crèches and family support. Many childcare settings now integrate care and education.

Visit the official website for Surestart's national childcare recruitment campaign at www.childcarecareers.gov.uk for information on careers and training opportunities working in early years, childcare and playwork.

You could be working as an **early years/nursery teacher**, fostering and developing the abilities, social skills and understanding of children aged 3 to 5. Early years/nursery teachers organise the learning environment within the nursery. They develop and implement work schemes and lesson plans in line with the requirements of the foundation stage. They help children to achieve their early learning goals and prepare them for their move to primary school education. Their work involves assessing, recording and reporting on the development and progress of pupils. They need to communicate and consult with parents and other professionals.

DID YOU KNOW?

64% of 3- and 4-year-olds are enrolled in pre-compulsory early years education, compared with only 20% in 1971.

Source: Office for National Statistics

Early years practitioners/nursery workers care for children up to the age of 5 in day nurseries, nursery schools, primary schools or hospitals. Early years practitioners help children to develop and learn through activities like play, counting games, storytelling and outings. They encourage children to develop language, number and social skills. Their work also involves observing and assessing children and producing reports on their development. In a day nursery they will also be responsible for caring for babies, including feeding and dressing. They need to make sure that children are safe at all times. **Early years professionals** are graduates who have gained Early Years Professional Status to become leaders in children's centres and full day care settings. They are role models to other people working in the sector.

Pre-school workers work in pre-schools or playgroups. **Pre-school leaders** manage staff and plan for the needs of children attending the pre-school. They provide care and education for young children, implementing programmes of activities suitable to their age range. They need to have an appropriate Level 3 qualification.

Pre-school assistants help the play leader and their work is similar to that of a nursery assistant.

Playworkers work in out-of-school clubs, breakfast clubs and holiday playschemes. They work with children from age 4 to 14. They plan, organise and supervise a range of play activities including sports, drama, music, arts and crafts, and cooking. They aim to provide a safe place for children to play. They may work in schools, community centres, faith centres or youth clubs. For more information visit www.skillsactive.com/playwork.

Nannies and **childminders** work in home-based childcare settings. Nannies are employed by families (normally working parents) to care for their children in the family home in either a live-in or live-out basis. They may also be expected to offer two or three evenings' babysitting each week. Childminders are self-employed and usually care for children in their own home. Nannies and childminders work with children of all ages, providing plenty of fun and learning opportunities within a safe environment. They work largely unsupervised. For more information visit the National Childminding Association website at www.ncma.org.uk.

CHILDREN'S SOCIAL CARE

Children's social care provides a range of care and support for children and families. This includes families where children are assessed as being in need, children who may be suffering 'significant harm', children who require looking after by the local authority (through fostering or residential care), and children who are placed for adoption.

Visit the social work careers website at www.socialworkcareers.co.uk for information about getting into social work. The General Social Care Council (which regulates social care workers and regulates their training) has information at www.gssc.org.uk about careers in social care and social work.

Children's and families social workers work in specialist teams and the work varies depending on the nature of the team. They may be providing assistance and advice to keep families together, managing adoption and foster care processes, or providing support to young people in the care system and leaving care. They work with children and young people at risk, as well as those in care to plan for their futures. Social workers respond to requests for help from families and children or young people. They also respond to referrals from other agencies or members of the community concerned about the welfare of a child. They aim to resolve problems within the family and promote the well-being of the children involved. Local authorities employ most children's and families' social workers.

Family support workers visit families in their homes who are experiencing difficulties. They offer practical help and emotional support. Their main concern is the care of the children. Difficulties rise from a variety of reasons, from financial and marital to problems due to the misuse of drugs or alcohol. Families are referred by social workers who may make recommendations. This may involve the family support worker encouraging and supporting parents in tasks such as bathing, clothing and feeding children appropriately, dealing with behavioural problems, and playing with the children. They also help parents to develop their parenting skills.

DID YOU KNOW?

The average age for someone leaving home is 24, compared with 17 for someone leaving care.
Source: A National Voice website
www.anationalvoice.org

Children's home managers are responsible for managing residential homes for children who are looked after by the local authority. They are employed either by the local authority or by homes run by the independent sector. You would be responsible for the welfare of children, managing staff and overseeing the administration and financial aspects of the home. Managers coordinate the home's work with social, education and health services supporting the children and their families. They may provide support to children and their families, develop programmes to promote positive behaviour, and contribute to care planning, statutory case reviews, and case conferences.

Residential childcare workers provide care and support to children and young people in children's homes, care homes, hostels and therapeutic services. They aim to promote a caring, safe, happy and secure environment for the children in their care. They assess children's social, emotional, physical, intellectual and cultural needs and plan and implement programmes that meet these needs. Typical duties include: maintaining daily care for the children, for example preparing meals and shopping, supporting various aspects of home life; liaising with related professionals; and arranging home/family visits. They work flexible shifts, including nights, bank holidays and weekends.

Care assistants, also known as care workers, work in residential homes where children with special needs such as severe disability require practical help with personal care. Their work typically involves helping children with personal care such as washing, dressing and feeding themselves, organising leisure activities and escorting children on outings.

Foster carers look after children who cannot live with their own parents due to problems at home. They provide a temporary home and family life. As a foster carer you would be responsible for providing a good standard of care and for providing a stable environment where children feel safe and wanted. Foster carers may provide emergency care for a few nights, short-term care for a few weeks or months, or long-term care for a number of years. They may also provide short breaks for families with children with special needs, disabled children or children with behavioural difficulties. Visit the Fostering Network at www.fostering.net for more information.

Portage workers work with pre-school children who have physical disabilities, developmental or learning difficulties, or other special needs. They visit children in their own homes and help parents to encourage their child's development through suggesting activities to make learning fun. They identify children's strengths and goals for future learning, and visit weekly to check on progress. They work with the parents to develop long-term goals. They aim to encourage full participation in day-to-day life within the family and wider community. For more information visit www.portage.org.uk.

THE CHILDREN AND FAMILY COURT AND ADVISORY SUPPORT SERVICE (CAFCASS)

CAFCASS is a public body which safeguards and promotes the interests of children involved in family court proceedings as defined by the Children Act. **Family court advisers** assess the needs of children and provide reports to the court reflecting the wishes and feelings of the child. They aim to make sure that the well-being and safety of the child is protected. **Family support workers** work with children and families to help them overcome problems with contact arrangements. They aim to help parents cooperate better and reach agreements.

YOUTH JUSTICE

The principal aim of the youth justice system is to prevent offending by children and young people aged 10–17 years. **Youth**

Offending Teams (YOTs) were introduced in 2000 to coordinate provision at local level to deliver this aim. Each team is led by a YOT manager and is made up of different members of staff who often work in specialist areas, such as substance misuse, accommodation or education and training. Job titles vary, including **youth justice officer** and **youth offending team officer/worker.** The work is wide ranging and may involve, for example, delivering intervention programmes for young people who have received a final warning from the police and carrying out assessments to determine factors such as why the young person has offended.

> **DID YOU KNOW?**
>
> In 2007–2008, a total of 87,400 children and young people aged 10–17 years old, entered the criminal justice system for the first time.
> Source: Office for National Statistics

Other jobs within the field of youth justice include the roles of **custody officer** or **care officer** within one of the three types of secure accommodation (secure training centres, secure children's homes and young offender institutions) for children and young people who have been sentenced to custody. Visit the YJB website for more information on work in this sector at www.yjb.gov.uk.

YOUNG PEOPLE'S WORKFORCE

The 'young people's workforce' (as defined by the Children's Workforce Development Council) covers workers working in a variety of settings, such as schools and community centres, primarily with 13–19-year-olds in a supportive role.

Education welfare officers or **attendance officers** aim to improve the attendance of children and young people at school. Poor attendance can be caused by many different factors, from family, health and psychological problems through to bullying or being

---

DID YOU KNOW?

In 2006/7 there were 8,680 permanent exclusions from primary, secondary and special schools.

Source: Office for National Statistics

---

unable to cope with schoolwork. You would be working with schools, children, their parents, carers and other agencies to promote school attendance, deal with absenteeism, and help children at risk of exclusion.

Connexions personal advisers (PAs) provide a free information, advice and guidance (including careers advice and guidance) service to all 13–19-year-olds. They aim to help young people make a smooth transition into adulthood and working life. You would also deliver individual support to young people who are not in education, employment or training, assisting them to overcome barriers to learning. You would provide advice on specialist issues such as substance misuse or housing. PAs work closely with schools, colleges, training institutions and employers to coordinate support for young people.

Learning mentors work with school pupils and college students to overcome barriers to learning and help them reach their full potential. They provide direct support with study skills, personal organisation and revision techniques. They agree targets for attendance, timekeeping and homework. They may also assist with confidence building exercises and anti-bullying strategies. You would be working with pupils one-to-one or in small groups. You would also work closely with teachers and other professionals as well as pupil's families. Roles and job titles regarding this kind of pupil support vary between different schools. In some schools, for example, the role may have more of an emphasis on behaviour support.

Youth workers and **youth support workers** work with young people aged 13–19 in youth clubs, faith centres, schools and community centres. You may be involved in organising fun activities, such as art, drama or sports, organising outings, or supporting young people to develop projects. Youth workers are employed in a wide range of job roles relating to substance misuse work and drug rehabilitation, housing, health and emotional well-being working, or even as outdoor sports leaders. Your role would be to help young people with their personal, social and educational development, and to support them to reach their full potential. Visit the National Youth Agency website at www.nya.org.uk for further information.

SCHOOL WORKFORCE

There are many other support roles in schools apart from those mentioned above. The following roles are a few examples of jobs where, like in the case of a learning mentor, you would be employed directly by a school. The Training and Development Agency for Schools (TDA) is the national agency responsible for the training and development of the school workforce. Visit their website at www.tda.gov.uk for further information on support staff roles in schools.

Learning support staff work with teachers in the classroom, helping pupils progress with their learning. They include **teaching assistants** and **higher level teaching assistants.**

Teaching assistants may work supporting an individual or a group of pupils, or they may support the teacher in the classroom. In nursery or primary school their tasks may include preparing the classroom for lessons, planning learning activities with teachers, helping pupils who need extra support to complete tasks, listening to pupils read or reading to them, and looking after children who are upset. Some schools employ teaching assistants with a specialism, such as English as an additional language, literacy or special educational needs. Most teaching assistants in secondary schools work as special needs assistants.

Teaching assistants may progress their careers through working towards Higher Level Teaching Assistant status. **Higher level teaching assistants** work right across the curriculum, acting as a specialist assistant for a specific subject or department or helping to plan lessons and develop support materials. They may also be expected to take classes.

Midday supervisors look after the welfare of school pupils in the dinner hall and playground during lunchtimes. They supervise pupils in the dining room and other parts of the school, helping clear away food and stack chairs and tables, and make sure pupils don't leave the school premises. They also resolve behaviour problems or report problems to the duty teacher.

Parent support advisers work with parents and/or carers and children to help improve behaviour and attendance and overcome barriers to learning. They work with parents to increase their involvement in their child's education, both at home and at school. Their work may include arranging and running classes for parents, giving one-to-one assistance to parents, contacting parents of absent students, and promoting attendance at parents' evenings.

EDUCATIONAL PSYCHOLOGY

Educational psychologists deal with the problems encountered by children and young people in education. This may involve learning difficulties, social or emotional problems. They make assessments of children's needs through consulting with colleagues and observing and interviewing the child. They then make recommendations on how to improve learning, for example through a learning programme. They also develop and support therapeutic and behaviour management programmes. Most educational psychologists work for local authorities. Visit www.bps.org.uk for further information.

HEALTH

Children's nurses work with children and young people who are suffering from a wide variety of conditions, from babies born with heart complications to teenagers with broken bones. They work in hospitals, child health clinics, day care centres and in the child's home. You may be treating patients and observing their progress, reassuring patients who may be confused or frightened, and supporting patients' families and carers. They may do shift work to provide 24-hour care.

School nurses work with children and young people in schools with the aim of promoting health. They are employed by local health authorities, community trusts and by individual schools. You may be providing health and sex education, providing health screening, and supporting pupils with conditions such as diabetes or mental health problems. You would work with schools to address concerns such as smoking, substance misuse or safe sex.

Health visitors aim to promote health and prevent illness. They work in a range of settings in the community including health centres, GP surgeries and people's homes. They work with mothers of babies and young children advising them on issues such as feeding, sleeping, safety, physical and emotional development, and managing difficult behaviour. They may also work with elderly people, people with disabilities and people with long-term illnesses, advising on issues such as diet and exercise.

DID YOU KNOW?

30% of children aged 2–15 years are classed as being overweight or obese.
Source: Health Survey for England (2007)

Midwives offer individual care to pregnant women and their families, helping women to take part in their own care during pregnancy. You would be supporting women from the confirmation of pregnancy through to the post-natal period (for not less than 10 days after the end of labour). You may be involved in talking through what to expect at various stages of pregnancy, running antenatal classes, teaching the skills needed to care for young babies, and looking after the mother and baby during labour and birth.

Hospital play specialists organise and supervise play programmes for children in hospitals or in hospices. They may also work with children with disabilities who are being cared for at home. They plan games and activities, help children settle in to the hospital, observe children as they play, and support families and siblings. They aim to help children cope with pain or feelings of fear or insecurity. Most hospital play workers work for the National Health Service (NHS), so visit the NHS Careers website at www.nhscareers.nhs.uk for detailed information on careers in the NHS in England.

This chapter has covered what you would be doing in a variety of jobs within the children's workforce, but what about career opportunities within the different sectors?

With the government commitment to improving standards across the whole of the workforce new qualifications have been and are being developed to allow career progression and continuing professional development in all areas, and so opportunities for progression are very good. See Chapter 10 (Training and Qualifications) for further information on entry requirements, training, and qualifications available within the different sectors.

As you can see, a great variety of roles are available within the children's workforce, so there's probably a niche somewhere for your own particular skills and abilities.

CHAPTER 7
CASE STUDY 3

PAULETTE OTETE

Childminder/Volunteer Classroom Support Assistant

Paulette Otete is a self-employed childminder, working from home. She is also taking further qualifications with the aim of becoming a qualified primary school teacher.

Paulette is currently responsible for childminding seven children, between the ages of 5 and 12 years old, together with caring for her own daughter aged 9. She picks the children up from school at 3pm and looks after them until their parents arrive to pick them up, often around 6pm. She is also available during the school holidays and at weekends.

Paulette sees the main role of a childminder as: 'You take care of the child, care in every way. This involves, for example, looking after their social, behavioural, physical and emotional needs, as well as their dietary requirements such as making sure they have something nutritional to eat when they come in.

'I have to plan all the activities I'm going to do with the children. You have to be flexible as this depends what they've been doing at school during the day, what homework they come back with and the ages and group dynamics of the children. If they are the same age group they often enjoy doing things together, but then I may bring the whole group together for a fun activity such as painting.'

Activities may involve stimulating learning activities, such as creative play or reading, or outdoor play, such as riding bikes, playing football, and trips to the park for physical activity. As Paulette's main age group is between 7 and 10 years then supporting the children with their homework is a key activity, especially if they are struggling in a particular area such as numeracy or literacy. This may be followed by the children having a quiet time and simply relaxing and watching TV or playing on the computer.

Paulette stresses the importance of looking at each child's individual needs in terms of their development. On the emotional side, for example, she will talk to the children about what they have been doing at school and, if they have been upset, she will then relay information from the teacher to the parents. On the social side she will monitor behaviour and discuss concerns with parents. If a child is shy, for example, she may suggest the child spends more time in an after-school setting rather than a home setting in order to further develop their social skills.

Paulette became a registered childminder when her own daughter was 3 years old. Her background is in social care, previously working as a nursing assistant with elderly clients in a private nursing home and with adults with a learning disability in the community. It made sense to switch to childminding and combine working with caring for her daughter. 'What I like about the job is the flexibility, and I've been able to study around it and gain further qualifications as well as being there for my daughter.'

After taking a BTEC Level 2 in Childcare Practice and registering to become a childminder Paulette became more interested in developing her own career and so went on to take a BTEC Level 3 in Childcare and Education. 'The course involved a number of placements in different settings including working in a private home with a baby, in a nursery, in a reception class and then in older classes within primary school. I could also combine this with childminding as I was working with 0–8-year-olds and could be assessed as part of the course in terms of what I was doing in my job.'

During this course Paulette became more interested in the education side and decided to become a primary school teacher. She has nearly completed a Foundation degree in Supported Learning. This course (as she is a childminder and not employed in a school as a classroom support assistant) has included voluntary work experience in primary school settings in order to achieve the work-based learning element of the course and to put what she is learning into practice.

Paulette works alongside the classroom teacher and teaching assistants with the role of supporting children's learning. This involves meeting with the teacher and discussing what is planned for the day. She may be asked to support a child individually, work with a small group of children or work generally within the class.

'I could be working one-to-one with a child with English as an additional language who needs literacy support in the classroom or be listening to a child read. Alternatively I could be working with a group of children who are struggling with an aspect of numeracy, such as the times tables. I encourage them to use different strategies and techniques. At the end of the day, it's very satisfying to see a child break through a barrier and achieve something they didn't think they could do.

'Supporting children in the classroom and working as a childminder need similar skills such as patience and tolerance. In the classroom you also need to develop your behaviour management skills. You need to be able to deal with children with behaviour disorders, as well as dealing with the emotional behaviour of children from a variety of backgrounds, and children who are generally misbehaving.

'As a childminder you're focusing attention on the child on a one-to-one basis in the home, rather than in a large group, which is obviously more relaxed. Also I like the fact that I can make my own decisions, as I'm not accountable to anyone, apart from the child's parents!'

The Foundation degree leads to the final year of an Honours degree in Education Studies, after which Paulette intends to take a one-year Postgraduate Certificate in Education (PGCE) before being able to take up a teaching post.

Paulette's tips to anyone looking to work with children are: 'Any kind of hands-on work experience is really useful. Think about doing some voluntary work in a school or a nursery, or taking a course that will involve some work experience.'

CHAPTER 8
FAQs

By now you should have a much better idea of what working in the children's workforce is all about and the varied opportunities it can offer. The descriptions of the different types of jobs available may help you decide what kind of work with children and young people you'd like to do, for example whether you'd prefer to work with babies and young children or teenagers and young adults, and whether you'd prefer to work in a social care or health setting. But what about other things you need to consider? Who will you work for and where will you work? What kind of salary could you expect to earn? Even more importantly, how will it affect your career prospects? In this chapter we look at some of the most commonly asked questions about getting a job in the children's workforce and the benefits it can bring to you personally. This should help you decide whether or not this is a career path you wish to follow.

Q Will I have pre-employment checks?

A Yes, pre-employment checks are really important in the children's workforce, as employers have a duty to safeguard those with whom they work. You will be in a position where you will be responsible for the welfare of children and young people and it is therefore vital that your employer can check that you do not have criminal convictions that might suggest you are not suitable for this kind of work. You will be asked to provide references and to undergo a Criminal Records Bureau (CRB) Disclosure. You will also be checked against the Protection of Children Act (PoCA) List, which names individuals who are considered unsuitable to work with children.

CRIMINAL RECORDS BUREAU

The Criminal Records Bureau (CRB) is an Executive Agency of the Home Office. It acts as a one-stop-shop for organisations, checking police records and, in relevant cases, information held by the Department of Health and the Department for Children, Schools and Families. The CRB was launched in 2002 to help organisations to make safer recruitment decisions.

Source: CRB website www.crb.gov.uk

Who will I work for?

Work in this area covers a huge amount of different organisations. You could be working in the public sector, the private sector or the third sector (which includes charities, not-for-profit organisations and voluntary organisations). Early years practitioners, for example, may work in the public sector for a local authority, in the private sector for an independent school, or in the third sector for a not-for-profit organisation such as a pre-school. They may also be self-employed as childminders or work for private individuals as a nanny.

Local authorities are a major employer. They employ social workers, family support workers, residential carers, support staff, portage workers, education welfare officers, educational psychologists, youth workers, and staff in children's centres, nurseries and schools.

Other possible employers might include the following.

▶ **Primary Care Trusts** – employing midwives, health visitors, children's nurses and school nurses.

▶ **Private organisations** – such as independent fostering agencies, residential establishments, independent schools and day nurseries.

▶ **Agencies** – recruitment agencies specialising in social care, nursing, and early years, childcare and education.

▶ **Government agencies** – such as CAFCASS, the Youth Justice Service and Connexions.

▶ **Voluntary organisations,** not-for-profit organisations, faith organisations, local charities, and national charities such as Barnardo's and the NSPCC.

Q **Where will I work?**

A You could be working in a wide range of settings, including:

▶ pre-schools and crèches

▶ day nurseries, nursery schools and primary schools

▶ out-of-school clubs and holiday playschemes

▶ secondary schools and colleges of further education

▶ hospitals, health centres and children's centres

▶ residential children's homes and schools

▶ community centres, youth clubs and drop-in centres

▶ private homes or your own home.

Q **Who will I work with?**

A Your colleagues will vary depending on your particular job but you will normally be part of a team working closely with other agencies and organisations on behalf of children and young people. For example, you may need to liaise with health professionals, council departments, social services, schools, the courts, and the police service. You will have direct contact with parents and carers and in some roles, for example portage workers and family support workers, you will be working closely with them.

Q **Will I work 9 to 5?**

A Again, this will vary widely depending on your particular job and the setting you are working in. As a full-time employee within a local authority you would work a standard 37-hour week, often with flexible working hours and opportunities for part-time and job share. In many jobs, however, particularly professional jobs, there

49

would be an expectation to work additional hours as and when required. Social workers, for example, may have to visit a child in the evening and teachers need to attend events such as parents' evenings.

Many people in the children's workforce work part-time. This is particularly the case within early years settings such as pre-schools and out-of-school clubs with limited opening hours. Many also work on short-term temporary contracts, for example playworkers on a holiday playscheme. Some support staff in schools are contracted to work within the school day and within term-time only. Childminders, however, have the flexibility to choose their own hours, as they are self-employed.

In some settings you will be working unsocial hours. Workers in residential children's homes and children's nurses in hospitals work early morning, late night and overnight shifts. Nursery staff in day nurseries may work on a rota to cover for opening the nursery at 7am and closing it at 7pm. Live-in nannies will be expected to babysit on evenings and weekends. Foster carers have no fixed hours and can potentially be working 24 hours a day, seven days a week, 365 days of the year.

DID YOU KNOW?

There are just over 72,500 children and young people looked after on any given day in the UK, over 51,000 (71%) of whom live with 43,000 foster families. The Fostering Network estimates that a further 10,000 foster carers are needed across the UK.

Source: The Fostering Network www.fostering.net

How much can I expect to earn?

The children's workforce spans many different sectors and employers and salaries can also vary between the private, public and third sectors. The following figures are therefore only a guide to some of the key jobs in the children's workforce:

Early years

Nursery workers' starting salaries may be around £10,000 a year. Childcare practitioners qualified to Level 3 typically earn between £13,000 and £18,000 a year depending on the setting. Salaries tend to be higher in nursery schools and primary schools. A newly qualified early years teacher may earn around £20,000 a year, rising to around £40,000 for a nursery head teacher. Senior managers in pre-school/playgroups may receive £8 per hour, and other childcare staff get between £5.80 and £6.80 per hour. The level of allowance that a foster carer receives depends on a number of factors, but foster carers now receive a minimum weekly allowance. Childminders set their own hourly rate per child. Live-in nannies may earn around £18,000 a year, and substantially higher in central London.

Children's social care

Local authority family support workers may start on around £16,000 rising to between £19,000 and £25,000 with experience. Portage workers start on around £15,000 rising to between £19,000 and £22,000 with experience. Residential workers in children's homes may earn between £19,000 and £27,000 depending upon qualifications and experience. Managers of children's homes may earn between £32,000 and £38,000 a year. Local authority social workers earn between £22,000 and £30,000 a year.

Young people's workforce

Qualified youth and community workers may start on around £19,000 a year, rising to £35,000 for senior posts. Salaries for learning mentors range from £16,000 to £29,000 with management responsibilities; and Connexions personal advisers range from £18,000 for a trainee to around £30,000 with experience. Experienced youth offending team officers and education welfare officers may also earn around £30,000.

School workforce

Teaching assistants may earn between £13,000 and £16,000 a year, and higher level teaching assistants up to £19,000. Midday supervisors may earn around £7.00 an hour. Parent support advisers may earn between £17,000 and £29,000 for senior posts.

Health

Children's nurses and school nurses may earn between £20,000 and £26,000 whereas midwives and health visitors earn between £24,000 and £32,000. Nurses, midwives and health visitors who are team managers may earn up to around £38,000.

Others

Assistant educational psychologists may earn around £25,000 rising to around £55,000 for educational psychologists in senior posts. Family court advisers earn between £28,000 and £33,000, rising up to £37,000 for service managers.

Q What can I expect to get out of the job personally?

A Working with children and young people can be an extremely rewarding and satisfying career. Whether you work with young children or teenagers, you will see how your work can make positive and effective change in their lives, both in the present and for the future. The work can also be very demanding so you will need to be motivated, focused and enthusiastic in your role.

Q What qualifications do I need?

A You may be able to start some jobs at entry-level without specific qualifications, but a formal qualification is increasingly becoming a requirement for many jobs working with children and young people. New qualifications are currently being developed to increase standards across the workforce and workers are increasingly expected to have qualifications or work towards them in the job.

For many jobs, such as Connexions PA or learning mentor, entry requirements vary widely between employers and a relevant qualification (varying from a Level 3 qualification to degree level) may be needed. For entry into other jobs, such as teaching and social work, a degree is needed. Entry, qualifications and training for different jobs are covered in Chapter 10 (Training and Qualifications).

Q Are there good opportunities?

A There are clear progression routes within all the sectors and in many areas opportunities to progress, through further training and qualifications, right through from entry-level positions to managerial and professional level posts. Within early years, for example, it is possible to advance from working as a supervised assistant to working as a qualified practitioner and eventually as an early years professional (with equivalent status to that of a qualified teacher). Within schools, learning support staff can progress to become qualified teachers, and within children's social care, workers can go on to train to become social workers.

It is also possible, with further training, to move across the sectors. With this in mind, City & Guilds have developed two 'transitional' qualifications at Level 3 for early years workers and playworkers. The aim is to support workers who have already gained a relevant Level 3 qualification to move from one sector to another. Also see, for example, Chapter 1 (Success Story), where Jacqueline decided to change career from early years to social work, and Chapter 7 (Case Study 3) where Paulette, who is currently a childminder, is taking further qualifications with the aim of becoming a primary school teacher.

Take a look at the Career Opportunities flowchart (overleaf) to get an idea of what level of qualification you'll need for a range of careers in the children's workforce, and how, through further training, you could progress.

CAREER OPPORTUNITIES

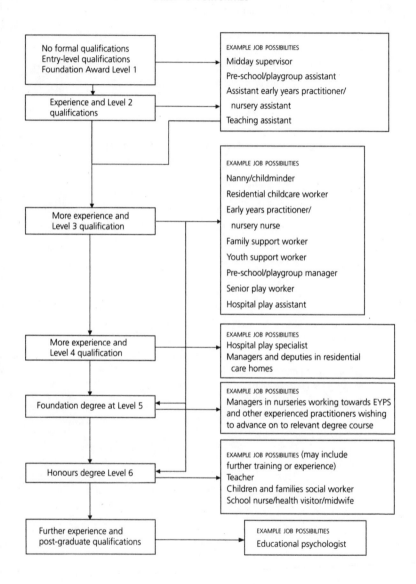

No formal qualifications
Entry-level qualifications
Foundation Award Level 1

Experience and Level 2 qualifications

EXAMPLE JOB POSSIBILITIES
Midday supervisor
Pre-school/playgroup assistant
Assistant early years practitioner/ nursery assistant
Teaching assistant

More experience and Level 3 qualification

EXAMPLE JOB POSSIBILITIES
Nanny/childminder
Residential childcare worker
Early years practitioner/ nursery nurse
Family support worker
Youth support worker
Pre-school/playgroup manager
Senior play worker
Hospital play assistant

More experience and Level 4 qualification

EXAMPLE JOB POSSIBILITIES
Hospital play specialist
Managers and deputies in residential care homes

Foundation degree at Level 5

EXAMPLE JOB POSSIBILITIES
Managers in nurseries working towards EYPS and other experienced practitioners wishing to advance on to relevant degree course

Honours degree Level 6

EXAMPLE JOB POSSIBILITIES (may include further training or experience)
Teacher
Children and families social worker
School nurse/health visitor/midwife

Further experience and post-graduate qualifications

EXAMPLE JOB POSSIBILITIES
Educational psychologist

CHAPTER 9
CASE STUDY 4

DAVE SCOTT

Student Support Officer

Dave Scott is a Student Support Officer at Fulford School, a large mixed comprehensive school in York. He is based in the student support office within the inclusion unit.

As a student support officer Dave's role is to offer support to students with social, behavioural and emotional problems. Problems can vary from, for example, a student with social problems who is lacking confidence and not coping in class to a student with behavioural problems who is disruptive in lessons. Dave, together with another student support officer, supports the Heads of Year and picks up and acts on problems as they happen.

'We find out what the problem is, then talk things through with the student. If it's a behavioural problem then it's important for them to understand that if they carry on misbehaving there will be punishments. If a student is being bullied then we'll speak to the people doing the bullying to sort the problem out. Depending on the problem, we may refer the student to another professional.'

Dave will target students identified by Heads of Year as needing support. If a student, for example, has organisational problems then Dave will make timetables for them which are easier to read, help them make notes in their planner, and maybe do a deal where they come in at lunch the next day to prove they have done their homework. 'We ask them to come in and see us at break or form time to have a chat about how things are going. We aim to build a relationship with them. Once we've built a rapport with them they then come to us with all sorts of problems.'

The job involves liaising with other professionals, such as the education welfare officer over attendance issues, the school nurse around health concerns, and Connexions' personal advisers who offer confidence building and anger management support. Dave is also a link between students, teachers and support staff. He will speak to teachers, for example if a student is struggling in their lessons, and keeps Heads of Year informed. He also has two-way communication with parents so everyone can stay informed.

Dave's job involves a lot of repair work. If a senior member of staff brings someone into inclusion he will calm the student down and help them write a statement about what's happened, for example breaking a window or being in a fight. His office is also available for students to come and see him for a chat if they are getting stressed out with their workload, or to come in and calm down if they have been upset in a lesson.

A challenging aspect to Dave's job is when a pupil joins the school after being excluded from another school. Dave will be responsible for easing them into the school routine. He will set a reduced timetable to start with, customise the timetable according to staff, offer support in lessons the pupil is struggling with and give lessons on a one-to-one basis.

Dave lost interest at school and college and ended up drifting into a number of unsatisfying jobs. He decided to do some voluntary work during his holidays and helped out in a classroom at Fulford School. He enjoyed this and when a teaching assistant post came up he applied and got it, supporting students with learning difficulties. He applied for his present job because he liked the idea of helping students not to make the mistakes he made. His own experiences have helped him to connect with students and to act as a role model.

The main qualities needed for his job, Dave feels, are: 'To be a good listener. You also need to be patient and keep your cool. You have to be approachable, be able to empathise and be able to give good advice. I see myself as being a real person who the students can come and speak to about anything and I'll work things through with them. You also need to be consistent, reliable and well organised.'

Dave is passionate about his job, 'What I love is that I can spend an hour or even just 10 minutes with someone and, at the end of the day, when they're walking out of school, they smile or wave and say thanks for that advice. I go away thinking I've made a difference and that gives me a sense of satisfaction. I'm trying to be a positive role model and like to help people have a better understanding. I'll often chat to students who've been messing around to try and change their mindset. I enjoy it – it's not really a job for me, it's part of my life. The only thing I don't like is the paperwork!'

Since working in the school Dave has taken an NVQ Level 3 while working as a teaching assistant, and is currently taking the National Programme for Specialist Leaders in Behaviour and Attendance (NPSLBA) at Level 3. This is a new programme designed to enhance the leadership skills and knowledge of professionals working in the field of behaviour and attendance. After this Dave will be able to go on to take a Foundation degree.

In terms of his career, Dave's current role is changing as the school is introducing a new tutoring system, which means his role will focus more on behaviour support than student support. There will also be the opportunity for Dave to have more input into how the job evolves. In the longer term, Dave can see himself working with more vulnerable, excluded young people ... 'But I would miss school!'

Dave's tips for anyone looking to go into this kind of work are: 'Do some voluntary work in a school. This way you'll find out if you enjoy it and also make some contacts too. Life experience is really important but you need to be able to listen too. You'll need an open mind and a willingness to continually learn. Never think you know it all!'

CHAPTER 10
TRAINING AND QUALIFICATIONS

So if you've now decided that working with children and young people is what you really want to do, and feel you have the necessary skills to make a successful career in this area, what's the next step? As you will know by now working in the children's workforce spans a number of different sectors and many different jobs. To help you decide which area of the children's workforce may be of interest to you, it's important to get an idea of the qualifications and training you might need.

This chapter therefore focuses on qualifications and training within the different sectors, from early years and children's social care through to youth and health. The qualifications you will need to gain will vary depending on which sector you choose to work in and the particular type of job you are interested in. As the children's workforce becomes increasingly recognised as a professional industry, however, a formal qualification is increasingly becoming a requirement for many jobs, and staff throughout the workforce are currently working towards qualifications at various levels.

For some jobs it is possible to enter without formal qualifications. Employers may look for personal qualities and experience of working with children rather than specific qualifications. This is particularly true if you are looking to start out in an unqualified, supervised role, such as an assistant childcare practitioner/nursery assistant, and then gain qualifications on the job. In order to progress, however, and for some college courses and apprenticeship schemes, it is an advantage (or a must) to have at least 4 or 5 GCSEs (A*–C), preferably including English, or the equivalent.

For other jobs you will need a higher-level qualification to apply, such as a diploma, degree or a post-graduate qualification. These jobs include early years professional, nursing, teaching and social work, and from 2010 will also include youth work.

While there may be no set entry requirements for certain jobs, many employers will be looking at your ability to receive on-the-job training and take further qualifications and therefore it is important to achieve the best qualifications you can while still at school. After school, you may also want to consider taking a relevant course at college, or you may decide to take an apprenticeship and gain qualifications on the job. Take a look at the following qualifications.

DIPLOMA IN SOCIETY, HEALTH AND DEVELOPMENT (SHD)

Diplomas are a new qualification for 14–19-year-olds that are becoming increasingly available in schools and colleges. They blend applied learning, academic study and hands-on experience in the workplace. They aim to provide young people with the skills and knowledge to set them on their way to finding a job or a route into higher education.

The Diploma in SHD has been available since September 2008. It is designed to provide young people with an understanding of health, community justice, social care and children's services and to help them develop the skills needed for working successfully in all these areas.

The Diploma in SHD is offered at Levels 1, 2 and 3 and is aimed at 14–19-year-olds of all abilities:

- Level 1 is equivalent to 4 or 5 GCSEs
- Level 2 is equivalent to 5 or 6 good GCSEs
- Level 3 is equivalent to 3 A levels.

Learners have 10 days' work placement at Levels 1 and 2, and 20 days' work placement in at least two sectors at Level 3.

SHD is flexible. Students can choose, for example, to combine the qualification with other GCSEs and A levels at Level 2 and 3. They can move on from SHD to an apprenticeship, employment, A levels or into higher education. The qualification also aims to give students an informed career choice by offering them a taster of four different work sectors. There is a wide range of jobs in the children's workforce that the SHD could lead to, from children's social worker to playworker, and from nurse to youth worker. For detailed information on the Diploma in SHD visit www.skillsforhealth.org.uk/diploma

QUALIFICATIONS IN CHILD STUDIES

The Council for Awards in Children's Care and Education (CACHE) is the UK's specialist awarding body for nationally recognised qualifications in childcare. They offer vocational qualifications at a range of levels, which you may be able to take at school or college, to prepare you for work in this sector. Each level acts as a stepping-stone to the next. You could, for example, work towards courses from Entry Level through to Foundation Level 1 and then onto Level 2. Visit their website at www.cache.org.uk for detailed information on all courses offered; the following are just a sample of these.

▶ The CACHE Level 2 Award/Certificate/Diploma in Child Care and Education prepares learners to work in a supervised capacity with children and families and is therefore suitable for people wanting to train as an assistant in a childcare setting, or go on to a Level 3 course.

▶ The CACHE Level 3 Award/Certificate/Diploma in Child Care and Education prepares learners to work unsupervised with children and families in a variety of settings. A similar Level 3 qualification offered at colleges is the BTEC National Diploma in Children's Care, Learning and Development. After these courses you could look for work, for example as an early years practitioner in a day nursery or as a classroom assistant, or progress onto higher education courses such as a Foundation degree in Early Years or into courses for nursing, teaching or social work.

QUALIFICATIONS IN HEALTH AND SOCIAL CARE

Vocational qualifications in health and social care are also available at various levels, providing a gateway to a variety of different careers and courses. A health and social care course at Level 2, for example, may lead to jobs such as health care assistant in a hospital or care setting, working with the elderly, disabled or with children, or may lead to a Level 3 qualification.

Level 3 courses offered at colleges include the:

▶ Vocational A level Health and Social Care (Single or Double Award)

▶ National Diploma in Health and Social Care.

Students can move on from these courses to higher education and degrees such as nursing, midwifery or teaching. Alternatively they can look directly for work in the health and social care sector. While you're still at school you may also be able to opt for a GCSE in Health and Social Care (Double Award) which will give you a good grounding in the subject.

APPRENTICESHIPS

If you're thinking about leaving school and going straight into the workplace then you may be interested in applying for an apprenticeship. Apprenticeships provide 16–24-year-olds with a mixture of on- and off-the-job training while they are being paid. As employees, apprentices work alongside experienced staff to gain job-specific skills. They also receive off-the-job training, usually on a day-release basis, with a local training provider (such as a college) to acquire the knowledge to underpin their practical skills.

An apprenticeship may take anything from 12 to 24 months or longer. Different apprenticeships have different entry requirements and you will need to discuss this with the training provider and employer. There are two levels of apprenticeships in England.

▶ **Apprenticeships at Level 2** – these are for people who wish to work towards an NVQ Level 2. They also offer an ideal pathway to Advanced Apprenticeships and further education programmes, which can help open up new career opportunities.

▶ **Advanced Apprenticeships at Level 3** – these are for people who wish to work towards an NVQ Level 3, and who show the ability to progress to positions at a supervisory level.

The following apprenticeships leading to jobs within the children's workforce may be available.

▶ **Children's Care, Learning and Development** – this apprenticeship is for people who work with children – from birth to 16 years – in settings or services whose main purpose is children's care, learning and development.

▶ **Youth Work** – this apprenticeship is about helping young people fulfil their potential through personal and social development. At the end of your apprenticeship you will be a youth support worker and in a good position to pursue a degree.

▶ **Community Justice** – in this apprenticeship you could focus on the youth justice pathway and be working with young people at risk of offending or re-offending. For more information visit www.skillsforjustice.com.

▶ **Playwork** – this apprenticeship is about providing out-of-school opportunities for play for children and young people aged between 4 and 16 years. Visit www.skillsactive.com/training/apprenticeships to find out more.

▶ **Supporting Teaching and Learning in Schools** – this apprenticeship is about providing support in the classroom. An Advanced Apprenticeship is a good stepping-stone to a Foundation degree or Higher Level Teaching Assistant Training.

For detailed information about apprenticeships visit www.apprenticeships.org.uk.

NATIONAL VOCATIONAL QUALIFICATIONS (NVQs)

You will study for NVQs if you are taking an apprenticeship. You will also be expected to work towards them in many jobs. NVQs (or Scottish Vocational Qualifications – SVQs) are work-based qualifications which show that you are competent to do your job and that you understand the reasoning behind the tasks you carry out. There are no exams – you are assessed for your NVQs while you work. They are available at different levels and in different subjects depending on your job role and responsibilities, right up to management level. The time taken to complete an NVQ is flexible, although on average they take a year. NVQs are available to full-time, part-time, paid and voluntary workers within the children's workforce.

CITY & GUILDS

City & Guilds is the leading award body in the UK, and the only awarding body solely dedicated to vocational learning, offering qualifications from Entry Level up to Level 7 (the equivalent of a postgraduate qualification). It has the most extensive range of children and young people qualifications available. Visit their website at www.cityandguilds.com to explore the range of subjects on offer. You can search for qualifications by the subjects, which are categorised into industry sectors. The following sectors may be of interest:

- Advice, Guidance and Counselling
- Children and Young People
- Community
- Education and Training
- Health and Social Care
- Health Science and Technology
- Justice.

The Children and Young People sector has links to qualifications for the following subject areas:

- children and young people services
- early years
- residential care
- youth work

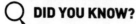

DID YOU KNOW?

The roots of City & Guilds can be traced back to the mid-thirteenth century when the livery companies of London began to form. They were originally developed to safeguard their specific trades, taking charge of everything from wages to labour conditions.
Source: City & Guilds
www.cityandguilds.com.

► youth justice

► parenting services

► playwork.

The website also has a career zone for learners (14–19) with information on levels and types of qualifications, as well as a section which gives you a broad idea of what's involved in a range of careers and what qualifications there are to get you started.

FOUNDATION DEGREES

Foundation degrees are a work-related higher education qualification. They combine academic study with work-based learning. They allow students already employed to study and get ahead in their career while working. Courses are delivered by colleges and universities and have flexible learning arrangements. They normally take two years full-time or three years part-time to complete. At the end of a foundation degree course students have the opportunity to continue, and 'top-up' to an Honours degree, which usually takes one year full-time or two years part-time. There are Foundation degrees relating to many job roles involving work with children and young people. For further information visit www.fdf.ac.uk.

JOB-SPECIFIC QUALIFICATIONS AND TRAINING

Take a look at the qualifications and training in the following sectors, which relates to the job roles previously outlined in Chapter 6 (What are the Jobs?).

Early years

Early years/nursery teachers in state primary schools/nursery schools need to have a degree and to have completed a period of initial teacher training to gain qualified teacher status (QTS). There are many different ways of getting into teaching. Visit the TDA website at www.tda.gov.uk for detailed information.

People working under supervision as assistants in early years settings may start by working towards NVQ Level 2 in Children's Care, Learning and Development. They may then go on to take NVQ Level 3 in Children's Care, Learning and Development and become qualified **early years practitioners**, able to work unsupervised and plan and organise their own work.

Once you've gained a Level 3 qualification there's very good scope for progression. You could move up into more senior positions and take further training and qualifications while working, such as an NVQ Level 4 in Children's Care, Learning and Development, a Level 4 Higher Professional Diploma in Early Years, or leadership and management training. You could also take a Foundation degree in Early Years, which could lead onto a related Honours degree. Once students have successfully completed their degree they can choose to work towards Early Years Professional (EYP) status or may decide to progress onto a further year's post-graduate study in order to gain Qualified Teacher Status (QTS).

By gaining EYP status you would become an **Early Years Professional**, leading work with children. EYP status is a Level 6 qualification for graduates. The Government's current commitment is to have a graduate-led early years workforce, and for every children's centre to employ an EYP by 2010 and every full daycare setting by 2015. In addition, all childcare workers will be encouraged to achieve at least an NVQ Level 3 qualification.

Most **playworkers** are trained on the job and work towards recognised qualifications in playwork, such as NVQs at Levels 2 and 3 in Playwork or the CACHE Certificate/Diploma in Playwork. There are also Foundation degrees and degrees in playwork. See www.skillsactive.com/training for further information. The Government wants to see the playwork workforce qualified to at least Level 3 where appropriate, and led by professionally trained graduates.

Nannies don't legally need to be qualified but in reality many agencies require a Level 3 childcare qualification as this ensures the nanny is capable of working in an unsupervised environment. All **childminders** must take an introductory childcare training course in home-based childcare and hold a paediatric first aid certificate as part of their registration. Childcarers wanting to develop their careers can take the CACHE Diploma in Home-based Childcare, a Level 3 qualification tailored especially to those providing care and education in a home-based setting. This course provides the 'underpinning knowledge' for the NVQ Level 3 in Children's Care, Learning and Development. They may then go on to take a relevant Foundation degree and higher-level qualifications.

Children's social care

To work as a qualified **children and families social worker** you would need an Honours degree in Social Work or an equivalent social work qualification. The full-time degree course lasts three years, but those with a degree already can apply to take a Masters degree in Social Work, which generally takes two years. The degree can also be studied part-time or via distance learning. If you have relevant work experience and the minimum entry requirements you can apply to the Regional Trainee Scheme, where students are employed and paid by a local authority while taking their degree. Practising social workers can then go on to take specialised post-graduate training as part of their professional development. See www.socialworkcareers.co.uk for further information.

To become a **family support worker** you may not need formal qualifications, but experience of working with children and families is usually required. Family support workers may work towards Health and Social Care NVQ Level 3 Children and Young People and can go on to take a Foundation degree in Professional Studies in Family Support. **Residential childcare workers** need a minimum of NVQ Level 3 before starting work in this environment, which could be gained through a placement in a residential care setting. For **foster carers** there is a three-stage training framework that covers pre-approval (training before they can start), induction and development. They can also work towards NVQ Level 3. Workers in these settings can choose to undertake professional training in order to progress. NVQ Level 4 in Leadership and Management for Care Services, for example, is aimed at managers, deputies and assistants who hold managerial responsibilities within care services. They may decide to progress onto a Foundation degree, or take a full-time or part-time degree in order to train to become social workers.

There is no standard entry requirement to start work as a **portage worker** but many people already have professional qualifications and may be teachers, social workers, nursery nurses, health visitors, speech therapists or nurses.

The Children and Family Court and Advisory Support Service (CAFCASS)

Family court advisers need to be qualified social workers with at least three years' post-qualifying experience with children and families or in child protection. **Family support workers** need a relevant qualification equivalent to NVQ Level 3 or above.

Youth justice

Youth justice officer roles within Youth Offending Teams vary and so do entry qualifications. They may need to hold a relevant NVQ at Level 3 or equivalent, or a relevant professional qualification such as a degree in social work, or a degree in youth work. There is no formal route to working as a **custody officer** and staff in custodial settings tend to come from all walks of life.

The Youth Justice Board (YJB) has developed a range of qualifications in youth justice to support the work of youth justice services, including a Professional Certificate in Effective Practice (Youth Justice) and a Foundation degree in Youth Justice.

DID YOU KNOW?

94% of young offenders in custody are male.

Source: Home Office

Young people's workforce

Local authorities employ **education welfare officers** and entry requirements vary. Some authorities require a professional qualification in social work, youth work, teaching or related field. Entrants to work as a **Connexions personal adviser** and as a **learning mentor** will be expected to have experience of working with young people and may also need a relevant degree or be educated to at least Level 3. NVQs at Level 3 and 4 in Learning, Development and Support Services, drawing on National Occupational Standards, have recently been developed to cover the work of staff in these areas. There are opportunities to progress onto relevant Foundation degrees and there is also a new degree in Learning, Development and Support Services.

There are no set academic requirements for entry to youth work as a **youth support worker** but you will need to commit yourself to a programme of training to achieve a qualification. There are two types of approved qualifications in youth work – Youth Support Worker (YSW) qualifications and the professional qualifications. To gain YSW qualifications, training may be towards either NVQs or VRQs (vocationally related qualifications) offered at Levels 2 and 3. Universities and colleges offer professional

DID YOU KNOW?

In 2006/7 two-thirds (66%) of pupils in year 11 complained that they had been bullied in the last three years.

Source: Office for National Statistics

qualifications. From 2010 all new professional qualifications will be at degree level or higher, and you will therefore need to have a degree to become a professional youth worker.

School workforce

Entry requirements for entry-level **teaching assistant** posts vary between schools. They usually need to have at least good reading, writing and numeracy skills as well as some relevant experience of working with children. Teaching assistants may work towards NVQ Levels 2 and 3 in Supporting Teaching and Learning in Schools and Higher Level Teaching Assistant status. With HLTA status, a Foundation degree or equivalent qualifications, teaching assistants can progress on to teacher training by taking a degree leading to Qualified Teacher Status (QTS). Some may follow a part-time course to achieve a teaching qualification and QTS while working.

Midday supervisors don't necessarily need formal qualifications as most training is on the job, but many schools would look for a Foundation Award in Caring for Children.

Parent support advisers come from a wide variety of backgrounds including education, social care, Connexions, Sure Start and health services. They undertake an initial training programme and may go on to access an accredited parent support adviser vocational qualification.

Educational psychologists need a degree in psychology accredited by the British Psychological Society followed by further experience and qualifications.

Health

To work as a nurse in the NHS you must be registered with the Nursing and Midwifery Council (NMC), which means you'll need a degree or diploma in nursing.

Children's nurses need to have a degree or diploma recognised by the Nursing and Midwifery Council (NMC), qualifying them in the children's branch of nursing.

> ## ○ DID YOU KNOW?
> In February 2009, the Government announced an extra £20.5 million to help young people get better access to contraception and support for teenagers and raise the awareness of the risks of unprotected sex.
> Source: DCSF

School nurses need to be registered nurses with experience after registration in areas such as health promotion, child protection and family planning. They can study towards a Specialist Community Public Health Nursing degree or post-graduate diploma with school nursing pathways, normally either one year full-time or two years part-time, to become specialist practitioners in this area.

Health visitors are registered nurses or midwives who have done further training. You'll need to qualify and work as a registered nurse or midwife before completing a degree-level training programme, which usually lasts one year full-time, to become a health visitor.

Midwives must hold a degree in midwifery (or if they are qualified nurses, have completed a pre-registration midwifery short course), which leads to registration with the NMC.

Many **hospital play specialists** start as hospital play assistants with an NVQ Level 3 relating to childcare. They can then work towards the Level 4 Diploma in Specialised Play for Sick Children and Young People or equivalent qualifications.

INTEGRATED QUALIFICATIONS FRAMEWORK

Work is under way to develop an Integrated Qualifications Framework (IQF) for people who work with, or would like to work with children, young people, and their families. It is designed to support the delivery of the five outcomes of Every Child Matters: Change for Children, putting children and young people at the heart of all services.

The IQF will be a set of approved qualifications that allows progression, continuing professional development and mobility across the whole workforce. It will be a comprehensive set of qualifications, up to and including degrees and post-graduate qualifications. It will also provide information on the qualifications available for new entrants to the workforce. The Children's Workforce Network is developing the IQF and work will be completed in 2010. Visit their website for further details at www.childrensworkforce.org.uk.

Take a look at the Access to the Children's Workforce flowchart to get an idea of the different routes, including vocational and academic, into a range of careers.

ACCESS TO THE CHILDREN'S WORKFORCE

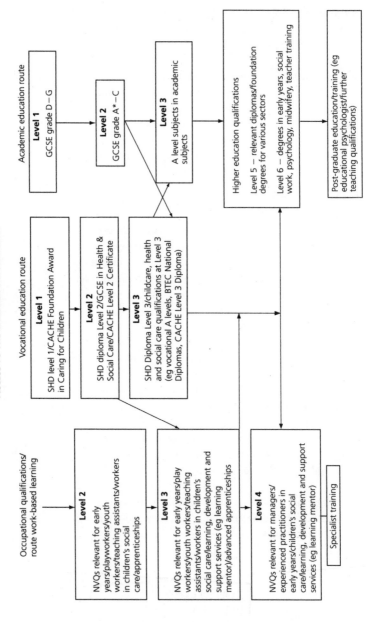

Academic education route

Level 1
GCSE grade D – G

Level 2
GCSE grade A* – C

Level 3
A level subjects in academic subjects

Higher education qualifications

Level 5 – relevant diplomas/foundation degrees for various sectors

Level 6 – degrees in early years, social work, psychology, midwifery, teacher training

Post-graduate education/training (eg educational psychologist/further teaching qualifications)

Vocational education route

Level 1
SHD level 1/CACHE Foundation Award in Caring for Children

Level 2
SHD diploma Level 2/GCSE in Health & Social Care/CACHE Level 2 Certificate

Level 3
SHD Diploma Level 3/childcare, health and social care qualifications at Level 3 (eg vocational A levels, BTEC National Diplomas, CACHE Level 3 Diploma)

Occupational qualifications/ route work-based learning

Level 2
NVQs relevant for early years/playworkers/youth workers/teaching assistants/workers in children's social care/apprenticeships

Level 3
NVQs relevant for early years/play workers/youth workers/teaching assistants/workers in children's social care/learning, development and support services (eg learning mentor)/advanced apprenticeships

Level 4
NVQs relevant for managers/ experienced practitioners in early years/children's social care/learning, development and support services (eg learning mentor)

Specialist training

CHAPTER 11
CASE STUDY 5

LYNN OWEN-JONES

Team Leader Children and Young People

Lynn Owen-Jones is a Team Leader for Children and Young People, working for Nottingham Community Health in partnership with Principia, a social enterprise that commissions health services for the community of Rushcliffe. She is based in West Bridgford Health Centre and is employed by Nottinghamshire County Primary Care Trust.

Her role is to manage staff within the central Rushcliffe area who are working in the children and young people's team. The team offers health services to children from ages 0–19 years, and is made up of school nurses, health visitors, healthcare assistants, nursery nurses and a paediatric staff nurse. The team has recently been formed with the aim of integrating the different services and building a supportive team around the needs of families.

As a team leader her job involves a mixture of line management, strategic work and some clinical work. Lynn's background is in nursing, most recently working as a school nurse, and she still enjoys going into schools and working with children and young people. This could be delivering a teaching session on a health promotion topic, doing health screening such as height, weight and vision screening, or doing routine vaccinations.

The role of a school nurse also involves a range of communication and liaison with other agencies, for example social care staff over a child protection concern, teaching staff about children with complex health needs, as well as related professionals such as educational psychologists, education welfare officers and other staff concerned with pupil support. School nurses attend multi-agency meetings, and can call a meeting if they have concerns about a child or take cases to joint access (multi-agency) teams if they are having difficulties accessing one or more agency to support a family.

Lynn always knew she wanted to work with children and was 17 when she started training to be a nurse. Once qualified, she worked as a staff nurse on paediatric wards in hospitals then decided to go into nurse education, as she enjoyed teaching and mentoring nurse trainees who came on the wards. She took a registered clinical teacher course and worked for a number of years as a clinical teacher.

The move to school nursing coincided with a family move to a new area and finding a nursing job which balanced alongside having young children of her own. She took a School Nurse Certificate at diploma level, gradually increased her hours to a full-time, term-time-only position before moving into a management role. Previously, she managed staff within the school nurses team in Rushcliffe before the children and young people's team was created and the services were integrated.

Lynn enjoys the variety of her job. As a line manager she has regular meetings with her staff, undertakes performance reviews and one-to-one staff appraisals, as well as supervising individual staff members' cases – in particular with regard to child protection issues. She also manages a budget and is responsible for staff recruitment and retention. On a strategic level, Lynn attends meetings concerned with developing the children's service, and looking at how her team is going to meet the targets and needs of the area. 'It's never boring! There's always more to learn and ways to personally develop.'

Lynn aims to carry on developing the team and working towards the challenges put their way. 'I think the idea of offering an integrated children's service is an excellent idea, as certain skills overlap. Sometimes there is joint working with a family between a health visitor involved with a new baby and a school nurse involved with an older child. I want to make sure that families have the right people with the right skills going in. If a health visitor or school nurse is not the best person, then we will refer to another agency. On the other hand, if one person is the right person, then they will become a key worker to the family and manage everything. We are trying to work in a more integrated way with all related agencies and professionals, accessing support for families from social care teams, paediatricians, GPs and clinical psychologists.'

The main skills and qualities Lynn feels that a school nurse needs are: 'You need to be very organised and a good communicator, including verbal and written skills, as well as teaching and counselling skills. You also need to be able to relate to children across the board, from primary aged children to teenagers in secondary schools. Clerical and IT skills are also a must. It's important for practitioners to keep up to date with their clinical skills, as families may ask for advice on anything from their child's medical condition to concerns over behaviour or bedwetting.'

Lynn's tips for someone wanting to become a school nurse are: 'Get the feel of whether you like working with children. Do some voluntary work, in a school or healthcare setting, or in a nursery or on a playscheme. During Year 11 apply to do your work experience in a school, perhaps working with the school nurse.'

'Also, if you want to have the opportunity to develop your career within the NHS, then my advice would be to take a nursing course at degree level rather than diploma level as there is a move to professionalise school nursing.' Current school nurses now have the opportunity to be seconded onto a specialist practitioner degree course – which Lynn has taken – in order to become a specialist community practitioner at a higher salary scale.

CHAPTER 12
THE LAST WORD

If you've gone to the trouble of picking up this book in the first place then you must have some interest in finding out what being a member of the children's workforce is all about. You'll have read about the positive changes happening within this workforce and the kind of skills and abilities that are needed to make a successful career out of working with children and young people. You'll also have read about jobs within the different sectors, the qualifications and training needed for them, and the range of excellent career opportunities.

Working with children and young people can be a very satisfying and rewarding career if you're the right person for the job. If you think you are and you'd like to find out more then Chapter 13 (Further Information) at the end of this book should help in your research. It lists websites of organisations representing the different sectors, useful careers and job hunting websites, and websites of volunteering organisations and major children's charities.

If you've decided that working with children and young people is what you really want to do, then the best way to find out if it definitely is the career for you is by doing some voluntary work. A huge range of volunteering opportunities are available, with a wide range of organisations and age groups, so it will also give you a better idea of the kind of work you are suited to. By volunteering

DID YOU KNOW?

National research on volunteering suggests that there may be around 2 million people engaged in formal volunteering across the children and young people's sector each month.
Source: National Centre for Social Research & Institute of Volunteering Research (2007)

you can also gain new friends and new personal skills through practical experience. You'll be giving your career a healthy kick-start, as the hands-on experience you'll gain will look really good on your CV. Whether you choose to volunteer with a local playscheme for children with disabilities or decide to become a mentor and give young people support and guidance, you could start to make a difference to someone else's life even sooner than you thought!

If you read the tips from the case studies then you'll remember that everyone's advice was to do some voluntary work. As Family Support Worker Jonny Hoyle said, 'Get some experience, do some voluntary work and see if you like it. Then really the sky's the limit – know where you want to end up and do whatever you can to get there.' And in terms of starting out in your career take Jacqueline Johnson's advice, 'Never give up. Have a plan of what you want to do and if you don't get it the first time, then try again. See every small step as a success and not a failure, because you have changed your life in a positive way. The more you widen your scope in life then nothing is wasted.' Good luck!

CHECKLIST

If you've made it this far through the book, then you should know that working with children and young people really is the career for you. Here's a final checklist to see if you're the right person for the job!

Tick Yes or No

Do you work well in a team?	☐ Yes	☐ No
Can you motivate and encourage others?	☐ Yes	☐ No
Do you want a career that challenges you?	☐ Yes	☐ No
Are you open and honest?	☐ Yes	☐ No
Are you a good communicator?	☐ Yes	☐ No
Are you a patient person?	☐ Yes	☐ No
Do you have respect for others?	☐ Yes	☐ No
Can you empathise with people?	☐ Yes	☐ No
Do you like taking responsibility?	☐ Yes	☐ No
Do you want to make a difference to people's lives?	☐ Yes	☐ No

If you answered 'YES' to all these questions then congratulations! You've chosen the right career. If you've answered 'NO' to any of these questions, then a career in the core children's workforce may not be for you. However, you may be suited to a job where you still come into contact with children and young people, for example in areas such as probation, policing, libraries, outdoor education, community education, hospitals, community health services, adult social care, and housing services.

CHAPTER 13
FURTHER INFORMATION

Children's Workforce Development Council (CWDC):
www.cwdcouncil.org.uk

This website has information on developments in the different sectors of the children's workforce relating to qualifications and training.

Early years

www.childcarecareers.gov.uk
This official website has information on careers and training opportunities for working in early years, childcare and playwork.

SkillsActive: www.skillsactive.com/playwork
SkillsActive is the sector skills council for Active Leisure and Learning. This website has information on careers, training and qualifications in playwork.

National Childminding Association (NCMA): www.ncma.org.uk
The NCMA is a charity and the professional association for nannies and childminders. This website has information on careers, training and qualifications for childminders and nannies.

National Day Nurseries Association (NDNA): www.ndna.org.uk
The NDNA is a charity and member association for nurseries.

Children's social care

General Social Care Council (GSCC): www.gssc.org.uk

The GSCC registers social care workers and regulates their training. This website has information on getting into social care work and social work. It has careers information for people thinking of going into social work, and lists accredited social work courses.

www.socialworkcareers.co.uk

This is the Department of Health's social work recruitment campaign website, with information about getting started in social work and applying for the social work degree.

www.socialcarecareers.co.uk

This is the Department of Health's social care website, with careers information relating to social care work.

CAFCASS: www.cafcass.gov.uk

This is the official website for CAFCASS with detailed information about the role of the organisation.

Youth justice

Youth Justice Board (YJB): www.yjb.gov.uk

The YJB is the official body which oversees the youth justice system in England and Wales. This website explains who they are and what they do and has information about Youth Offending Teams.

Skills for Justice: www.skillsforjustice.com

Skills for Justice is the sector skills council for the justice sector. Their website has information on careers and qualifications in this sector.

Youth work

National Youth Agency (NYA): www.nya.org.uk

The NYA aims to promote young people's personal and social development and give them a voice in society. Their website has careers information relating to youth work, including information on qualifications and training.

Schools

Training and Development Agency for Schools (TDA): www.tda.gov.uk
This official website has detailed information on careers in schools, including information on getting into teaching and training and career development for support staff.

Educational psychology

British Psychological Society: www.bps.org.uk
This website has information on careers in psychology, including training and qualifications.

Health

NHS Careers: www.nhscareers.nhs.uk
This website has detailed information on careers in the NHS in England. You can also search for current vacancies and apply online.

Nursing and Midwifery Council (NMC): www.nmc-uk.org
The NMC registers nurses and midwives. Their website has information on education standards and a search facility for NMC approved courses, programmes and institutions.

Careers and job hunting

Jobs4u: www.connexions-direct.gov.uk
This DCFS funded website is aimed at 13–19-year-olds and gives excellent information on jobs and careers. Click on the A–Z of Occupations to read profiles of jobs you may be interested in.

Children and Young People Now: www.cypnow.co.uk
Children and Young People Now is a magazine dedicated to those working with children, young people and their families. Their website has the latest news and job vacancies in health, social care, education, childcare, youth work and youth justice, as well as career tips, advice, and information on training and qualifications.

Guardian Jobs: http://jobs.guardian.co.uk
The Guardian Jobs site has careers advice, jobmatch and job vacancies.

Local government: www.lgcareers.com and www.lgjobs.com
The careers website has advice and information on careers in local government; the jobs website has current job vacancies in local government.

Jobsgopublic: www.jobsgopublic.com
On this website you can search for vacancies within the public and not-for-profit sectors.

Qualifications and training

Skills for Health: www.skillsforhealth.org.uk/diploma
Skills for Health is the sector skills council for the health sector. Their website provides detailed information about the Diploma in Society, Health and Development.

CACHE: www.cache.org.uk
This website has detailed information on all the childcare courses that CACHE offer.

Apprenticeships: www.apprenticeships.org.uk
This official apprenticeships website has detailed information for people wanting to know more about apprenticeships, including types of apprenticeships available. You can also search for, view, and apply for apprenticeships you might be interested in.

City & Guilds: www.cityandguilds.com
City & Guilds is the leading awarding body in the UK for vocational qualifications. Their comprehensive website has details of all the qualifications they offer.

Foundation degrees: www.fdf.ac.uk
This website lists all current available Foundation degrees and the institutions providing them. You can search for a course by subject or area.

Become instantly more attractive

To employers and further education providers
Whether you want to be an architect (Construction and
the Built Environment Diploma); a graphic designer
(Creative and Media Diploma); an automotive engineer
(Engineering Diploma); or a games programmer (IT
Diploma), we've got a Diploma to suit you. By taking our
Diplomas you'll develop essential skills and gain insight
into a number of industries. Visit our website to see
the 17 different Diplomas that will be available to you.
www.diplomainfo.org.uk

Volunteering

Do-IT: www.do-it.org.uk
This website is a national database of volunteering opportunities and you can search for local opportunities and apply online. It also has really useful information for anyone interested in volunteering, including tips to get started and volunteering blogs.

Volunteering England: www.volunteering.org.uk
This website has information on all aspects of volunteering. It gives advice on how to look for volunteer work as well as providing details of major organisations that place volunteers.

Community Service Volunteers (CSV): www.csv.org.uk/volunteer
Information about volunteering with CSV, the UK's largest volunteering and training organisation. CSV has full-time volunteering opportunities for young people who may want to take a gap year or gain experience for careers/courses in social work, health care, nursing, childcare, youth work, teaching or psychology. Placements last 4 to 12 months.

WorldWide Volunteering: www.wwv.org.uk
WorldWide Volunteering has a database of volunteering projects for people who want to find a UK or worldwide volunteer project.

Vinspired: www.vinspired.com
Vinspired is a community of 16–25-year-olds who do favours for free. Enter your location to search for local volunteer opportunities.

Children's charities

The following websites have information about these major charities, including volunteering opportunities with children and young people on a range of projects:

- ▶ The National Society for the Prevention of Cruelty to Children (NSPCC): www.nspcc.org.uk
- ▶ Childline: www.childline.org.uk
- ▶ Barnardo's: www.barnardos.org.uk
- ▶ Action for Children: www.actionforchildren.org.uk
- ▶ UNICEF: www.unicef.org.uk